FAST
FAST
FAST
FAST

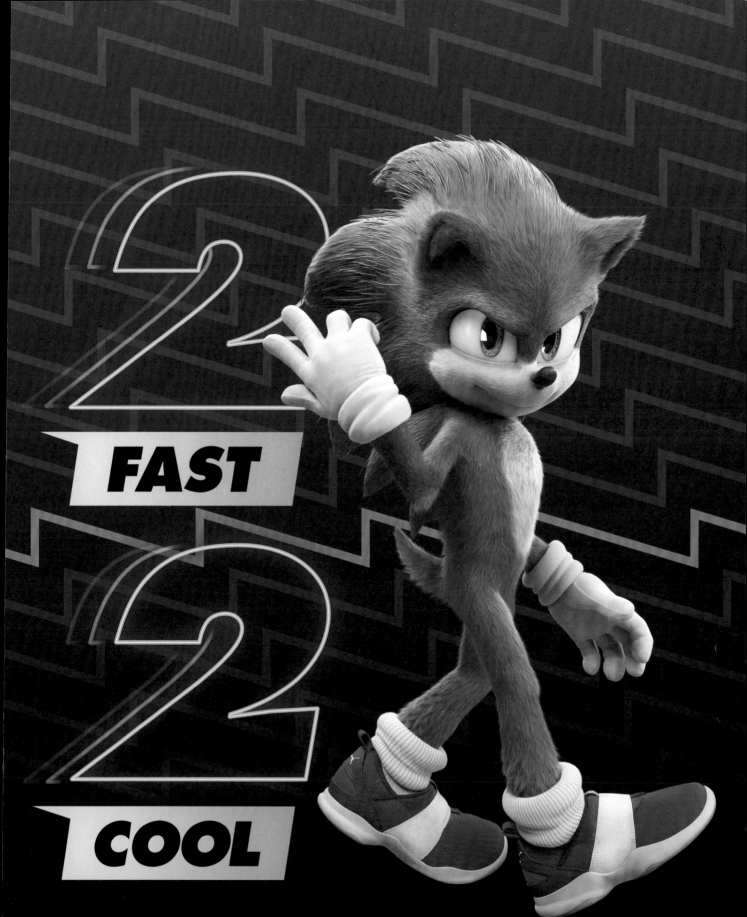

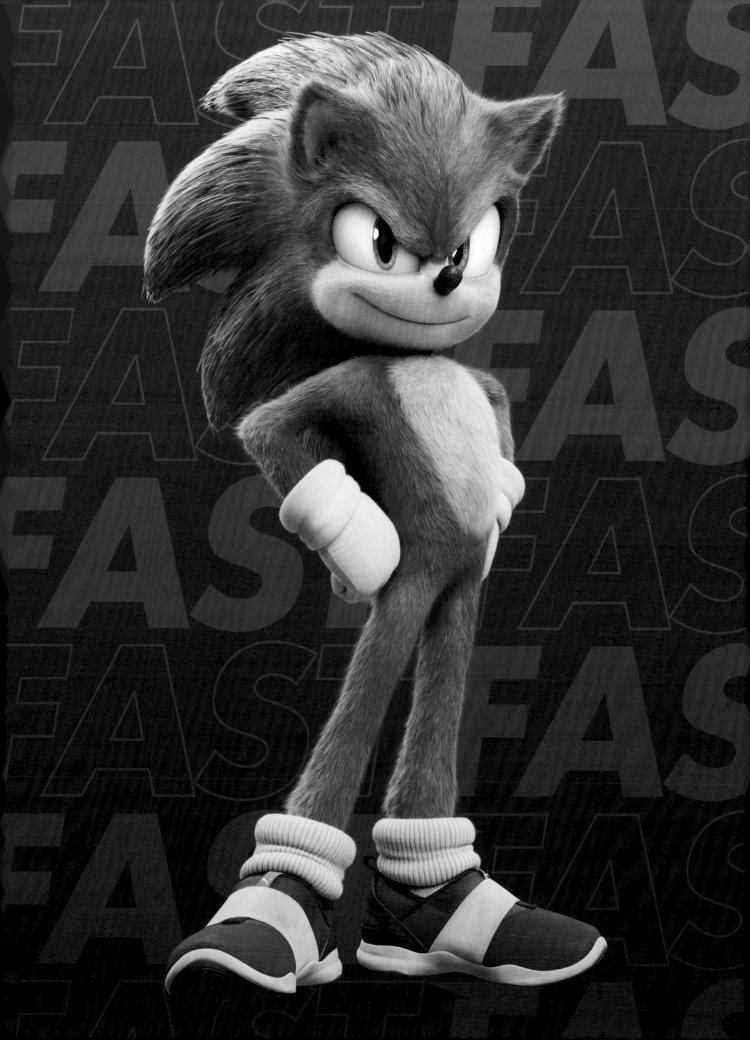

SONIC 2 THE HEDGEHOG

THE OFFICIAL MOVIE POSTER BOOK

GOTTA GO FAST!

12 ACTION-PACKED POSTERS INCLUDED!

 SEGA®

First published in the United States of America by Penguin Young Readers Licenses,
an imprint of Penguin Random House LLC, New York, 2022
Manufactured in Canada
ISBN 9780593387375
10 9 8 7 6 5 4 3 2 1
TC

$7.99 USA
($10.99 CAN)

PENGUIN YOUNG READERS LICENSES
Visit us at Penguin.com/kids

ISBN 978-0-593-38737-5

EAN

9 780593 387375

5 0 7 9 9 >

AGES 8-12